T0363083

The road to Tralfamadore

is bathed in river water

Blaise van Hecke

stories from a gypsy childhood

First published by Busybird Publishing 2018
Copyright © 2018 Blaise van Hecke
Copyright Illustrations © 2018 Jack Howlett

Paperback: 9781925830101
Hardback: 9781925830040
ebook: 9781925830033

Cover images: (Wadbilliga River): Blaise van Hecke;
(kids with dog): Lin van Hek
Photographs: Bath: Kev Howlett; Family in house: Mark Gillespie
Cover Design: Kev Howlett
Illustrations: Jack Howlett
Internal Design by Busybird Publishing

This is a memoir. Some names have been changed. The author reserves
the right to retell events as she recalls them and does not render them
as accurate facts.

A fictional version of 'Eleventh Summer' came second in the Society
of Women Writers Victoria, biannual short story competition in 2007
and was published in a short story anthology called *Mud Puddles* in
2008. 'Birth Day' was also published in *Mud Puddles* as fiction.

busybird

Busybird Publishing
2/118 Para Road
Montmorency Victoria
Australia 3094

A catalogue record for this
book is available from the
National Library of Australia

For Mama, the quintessential storyteller.

The Road

Will you come on a road trip with me?

It's just up the Princes Highway, about eight hours from Melbourne. The scenery hasn't changed much over the past forty-five years and we still sing out the same joke every time we pass Genoa at the border.

Genoa?

Nah, never met 'er.

Every. Single. Time.

We used to pick up hitchhikers (even though it was illegal) along the highway and eat hot chips, drowned in vinegar, in Lakes Entrance – the halfway mark. The car would be bursting with people, animals, bedding and food.

The turn-off is at a small highway town, called Cobargo. We'll follow some dirt roads, so wind up your window or you'll choke on the dust. It's picture perfect here and could be somewhere more exotic, like Switzerland. But this is dairy country. Home of Bega Cheese.

We're over the causeway now, starting the slow climb up the mountain. If we're lucky, we might see a dingo or a lyrebird. Can you feel the difference in the air? The crispness? The smell of eucalyptus? Take no notice of me if I smile like a crazy woman – it's the everlasting daisies scattered along the roadside: their yellow heads remind me that I'm almost home.

Okay, we're near the top.

To our left is the road that continues up to the fire tower. From there you can see the coast. If you're a fisherman, that's the place to go. The coast, that is. That's where you might see dolphins and whales. Serious fishermen (and women) come from all over the country to fish there. It's much more showy and glamorous, the sea, but it doesn't lure me.

Now we'll go down into the valley along this narrow, pitted road. This trip is excellent to work your core muscles, no gym membership needed, just hold on to your seat as we navigate the rugged terrain. Don't worry; my old Subaru has done this many times. I'll just put her into low-range gear. See, she's purring. Many non-four-wheel-drive vehicles try this trip but they don't handle it too well. There are five creek crossings but it'll be fine so long as they aren't flooded, or a tree hasn't fallen across the track. That's why we always carry a chainsaw.

After this last creek crossing, we pass 'the gate'. We're officially now on Tralfamadore. To our left is the Toucan Club – that's where Anando, Maddy, Bretski, Puj, Bhavana, and Dinesh lived. It was called Tent City first, then there was a fire and they had to rebuild.

As we follow the road along the ridge, we pass the Mine Flat. You can't see it from the road but Prem and Shree built their mud brick house down there.

A couple more valleys and turns and we'll pass the Sugar Shack. No one can agree on who built that place. Next to that is Dinesh's house. Then there's Margaret's place – which Nehar and Garimo built – down in the valley. You can't see it either but we'll walk over there some time. Near Margaret's is the school flat and the remains of the schoolhouse that never had school.

There's our place! Do you see it through the trees? Can you see how the creek curves around to join the river? We'll stop here first to say hello to the river. I always do.

Be still.

Listen.

Can you hear it?

It's my younger brothers, Billy and Couzie, and me in the creek bed. We're lean, naked and barefooted, monkeys scampering over the rocks. We laugh as we chuck stones into the creek, damming it up and taking tadpoles and small frogs as hostage. We'll spend all day building a fortress, the sun baking us. Our dog, Cloud, stands guard for a while before taking his woolly body into the shade.

There! Listen.

It's the creek gurgling underground at our feet. Up behind us is the house, an island with the creek on one side and the river on the other. There's Maddy and his sister, Anando, perched on river stones. Their wet skin glistens. They take a slow drag on a joint and nod to each other.

If you sit here for a while, you'll hear the clatter of children bombing into the clear water or spinning on an old tyre tube towards the rapids. There's laughter and banter as we champion each other in daring escapades. There might even be someone strumming a guitar, singing a folk song or two – the universal language of music wafting through the trees. We can follow these melodies into my dreams.

When I close my eyes, when I meditate, I always come to this spot. It flows through my veins. I'll come here when I die. I've left instructions with my sons to scatter my ashes into the water at this spot.

Without the river, I am nothing. This is where I come to be myself. This is the way.

The road to Tralfamadore is bathed in river water.

Call of the River

My mama was young when her first love died in a car accident. It left a large cavern in her heart and no daddy for her first baby, my big sister Sara. They were left to fend for themselves – wide eyed and innocent. They bought a house in North Carlton with the life insurance, and tried to get on with their lives.

My daddy was handsome and lovable but not good daddy material. Either that or the cavern was too big to navigate. Mama's heart just wasn't in it.

When I was barely able to walk, Mama, Sara and I left our house in Carlton, and sailed across rough waters, past the southern tip of Africa, on a ship from Perth to London. I don't know if we were following someone or leaving something but when we got to London, we sailed over to the continent to Belgium where the Flemish artists beckoned us.

Mama met Herman. He became our new daddy. We lived in a small cottage made from black and white bricks on a farmer's land. At night I slept in a hole in the wall; during the day I wandered in the snow in gumboots. Sara went to school and learned Flemish from the nuns while Mama and Herman lived the artist life. Herman was a painter, Mama was becoming one and all their friends were artists and writers. According to Mama the farmer's son often tied me to a tree. Mama also says that I would follow the farmer around in my tiny wooden clogs and made friends with a giant pig who also followed the farmer. But Mama likes stories and I never know fact from fiction.

We flew home to Australia a few years later with Herman, and my new chubby brother, Billy, in time for another little brother – blond and rambunctious – to tumble from Mama's body. In the outer suburbs of Melbourne we were a family of six blinking in the harsh Australian light. It seared our edges after living in the farmhouse in Ghent.

Our Flemish painter-father found it hard to get used to life in Australia. He went wandering with his paintbrushes to the south coast of New South Wales, where he made friends with other artists and gypsies. Mama, Sara, Billy, Couzie and I stayed at the outskirts of Melbourne in a rambling old weatherboard house at Cockatoo.

***

I was with Mama at the counter of the small supermarket in the one-street town of Cockatoo. Across the road was the doctor, the school a little further up the hill. But I wasn't old enough for school just yet.

I was with Mama (I don't know where my brothers were). She was talking to the lady at the checkout; my head was at the same level as the lollies. I fingered the packets, so pretty, so colourful. The box rattled when I shook it and put it in my pocket.

In the back of our Holden, I picked open the cardboard box and guzzled all the lollies, not having to share them with my brothers, or my sister.

On our way home, Mama and I went to the bottom of our steep hill on Salisbury Avenue and there, swimming in the clear water of the creek, turning in and out of the curls of water, playful and naughty was a platypus. Mama said it was good luck to see such a thing on my fifth birthday. I guess it was. I didn't know what luck was but it made me happy to watch the cheeky thing.

Later in the day my tummy hurt. The pain bent me in a tight ball, making me cry.

'What have you been eating?' asked Mama.

I shook my head, not understanding the question. We got back into the car and drove to the doctor.

A man with a white coat bent over me. 'Did you eat something you shouldn't?'

I frowned. 'Yes! Lollies.'

'Where did you get these lollies?' he asked and I pointed out the window to the supermarket across the street.

'Were these lollies red?'

'Yes.' There were red ones and other colours too. My voice didn't say this out loud. A lady came into the room with a branch, covered in red berries. 'Are these what you ate?'

I screwed up my face. Mama always said I shouldn't squint so much in case the wind changed but I couldn't help it. I was tired of all of these questions. My tummy hurt. I turned onto my side because it hurt less that way.

'Are these what you ate?' she asked again.

They whispered to each other and stopped asking me questions and eventually I fell asleep. I didn't like those lollies any more.

***

Mama took us to the coast to see our painter father. In our old green Holden, it was a long way along the Princes Highway, counting the white lines on the road, or playing *I spy*. We stopped in Lakes Entrance for hot chips with salt and vinegar and ate them straight out of the paper, on the grass beside the sea with the seagulls. You had to be on guard all the time with your food with two little brothers and those seagulls.

Mama drove all that way from Melbourne to a sea shack called The Nook near Bermagui. I don't know how she stayed awake so long while we snoozed in the back with our fortress of blankets and the smell of vinegar on our sticky fingers. At The Nook, we found our Flemish father and a cat called Mrs Black. It was crowded in the small house with our gruff daddy – the air was salty and the sea loud. It hushed us to sleep every night. *Shoosh, shoosh, shoosh.*

Each morning we followed Mama up a little hill to the main house – where a man named Bill lived – to milk the goat. The goat didn't like to be milked, her back legs kicking and her head thrashing. Sara and I collected twigs to start the fire while Mama tried to keep the metal bucket upright. Goat's milk is good, when you can get it.

Our painter father still didn't like Australia much so he went back to Ghent. Maybe he didn't like us much either because he didn't take us with him. We couldn't stay at The Nook because it was going to be pulled down. We lived in another shack nearby on the side of a cliff that someone said we could use. This house was made from driftwood and we kept adding to the walls with more pieces of driftwood as we collected it on the beach.

We could see sharks from up there and we'd wave to people swimming to warn them of the danger. They would wave back thinking that we were being friendly. They couldn't hear our warnings because the wind stole our voices as they flew off the cliff. We held our breath as we watched a shark fin circling nearby and let out our breath when it turned away from the swimmer.

The shack swayed in the wind and the *shooshing* of the sea wasn't as loud as down at The Nook. Mama made this our forever home but the locals didn't like it. They thought it was *obscene* that a woman lived there by herself, with all those children, no lights and no running water.

Our house was knocked over by a metal monster on wheels. We were allowed to take the carrots from the garden and all our pillows and clothes but now we were driftwood on the south coast of New South Wales.

This is where Mama met Jill. Jill lived at Tralfamadore but I didn't know where that was. It sounded far away and I wondered if we'd get chips with salt and vinegar on the way.

Jill drove us inland from the coast along a dirt road, across lots of river crossings, down into a valley, in her big four-wheel drive. The road was newly made, soft at the edges. Jill said a big tractor came through and moved everything out of the way. I wondered how the tractor driver knew where to go.

When we got to the river, it enchanted us. There were different noises here – not the crashing of the waves that shushed us all night long. It was louder than the city but quieter somehow. The bush tells you stories that you can't ignore.

Mama led us across the creek and up a little hill. *We will live here*, she said and I smiled.

We chased our little brother, Couzie, down the hill to where the creek meets the river, his white hair leading us. The creek gurgled and burped, egging us on. While Mama put up the tent, the river called us. Our big sister guarded us from danger, always.

I liked the big tent that Mama found. She said that it came from the army. It was as big as a house with two rooms and the dark green canvas flapped and creaked in the breeze. At night we could hear the frogs in the creek and so many un-named noises. There was no need to name them. They were there and we slept curled into each other, lulled by the dreaming of the bush and babble of the creek.

The River House

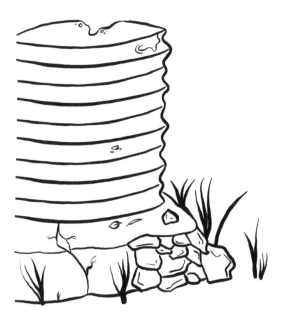

People arrived to build our house. I didn't know any of them but they were happy to see us.

'This is the way. Welcome to Tralfamadore,' said Jill.

Jill didn't really live at Tralfamadore. She lived on The Ranch with John. It was next to Tralfamadore but right up one end and was surrounded by cliffs. Everything was BIG at The Ranch. Big paddocks, big house, big tractor. John and Jill were like the King and Queen.

On our little island, a square of earth was marked out. We dug a spot at each corner (and some in between) using a crowbar because the earth was rocky. Hard to dig. Even the crowbar had trouble as it bit into the ground with a clunk and a scrape.

Everyone walked down to the river and up to the ridge at the top of the hill and scanned the trees. There were plenty of tall, straight gums to choose from. We just needed to make sure they were thick enough to use as uprights for our house. Too young and they were too spindly and unsteady.

We chose a handful and someone cut them, lining each tree along side the others on the ground, their stringy bark beginning to fray. We left the logs for a few weeks, until the bark started to come away from the wood. Then someone took the back of the axe to the log, pounding along the length of it. The bark separated from the log easily.

Us kids laughed and jumped up and down at the prospect of the bark coming away in strips, leaving the smooth creamy wood exposed and rough ribbons curling on the forest floor. The logs were carried down to the house ready for the building party.

The nude posts were set into the freshly dug holes, then set with concrete that was made from cement, sand and water. Mama decided that there were already two posts on site – two living trees – that she cut the top off and used as supports to the house. Some of the helpers frowned at this but carried on with other things.

Silver waves of roofing iron were placed over the upright posts, the front higher than the back so that water drained away. Our house started to take shape. The building party dusted off their hands, a job well done. They celebrated with food. Lots of food and home-brewed beer, wine, a bong or two and music. Music all night long. Guitar and drums, a few tambourines and Mama with her banjo. Mama singing, 'knockin on heaven's door'.

Sara, Billy, Couzie and I fell into bundles of sleep in the tent because the house wasn't ready to have us yet. It didn't matter because we were so tired from so much fresh air and working on the house.

Even though our car wasn't made for the rough roads, we'd go to town in our Holden, Mama putting her foot to the floor – *pedal to the metal* – to get up the steep hills. I knew we were going to town if we'd all had a bath in the morning and put on clean clothes.

In Cobargo, Mama went to the post office to collect our mail. There were usually envelopes with two-dollar notes in them from Granma Scott. She sent them to us every week no matter where we were. With this money, and dole money from everyone who lived in Tralfamadore, we'd buy big bags of oats, flour, milk powder and buckets of honey from the co-op in Bega. Sometimes Mama would buy dried apricots to have with custard, or sesame seeds to toast for breakfast. Milk powder was the best because when you mixed it with water, it didn't always dissolve properly and Billy, Couzie and I fought over the creamy lumps at the bottom of the jug. That was probably the only job that everyone wanted to do.

On our way home we went to the tip outside Cobargo to look at what other people threw away and filled the back of the car with old windows, doors and chairs. The car was always full of food, stuff from the tip, lots of kids and sometimes a dog or two, maybe even a chicken or goat. Luckily we had a roof rack on top. Mama really had to rev the car now that it was loaded up, to get over the mountain and across the rivers. We couldn't muck around on these trips because we had to concentrate and hold onto things if we wanted to get home in one piece.

When we got back to the river house, we unloaded our treasures and celebrated with lots of food, a bong or two, a big fire and music. Always music. *This is the way, welcome to Tralfamadore.*

The bonfire was huge and sat behind our house. People came from the bush, as if they lived in the trees, along the long straight track that we called The Saddle. It started from the back of our house, past the spotted gum and along the ridge towards Peter Pumpkin's house. It felt like walking along the back of a dragon, its tail stretching long after the end of the track and up the mountain.

The fire was always big. We sat around it, on the ground with crossed legs. We'd sing and sway to the music, along with the leaping flames. Dogs and kids ran in and out of the music, chasing each other until we couldn't stand up anymore. *She'll be coming 'round the mountain when she comes, oh Lord ...*

We slept piled in the tent. Our house still wasn't ready for us yet.

Mama worked on the house every day. She mixed cement with sand and water in a wheelbarrow and added a river rock to the wall, one at a time. Sometimes only five rocks might be added because we ran out of them and needed to collect more from the river – we tried to help but could only carry small rocks – or we ran out of cement and had to wait until we went to town for more. We collected coloured glass bottles and jars from the tip, or saved them from the food we bought. They made great walls that let in light and a rainbow of colours when the sun was setting.

Some of the walls were finished quickly when Mama found old stable doors that a farmer was getting rid of. Mama used them on one wall and we'd play with them, opening and closing them for hours. One of them became the front door. My favourite was the Volkswagen car door at the back of the house. The window winder still worked so we could open and close the window as much as we wanted. All Mama had to do was cement the door into the wall. When people came over we had to demonstrate how it worked. Over and over again.

Mama studied books on how to build a fireplace. John and Jill had a huge one up at The Ranch. When John cooked us pancakes, the stack of pancakes was huge too. Mama wanted our house to have a perfect fireplace, so every time we visited another house we had to talk about how to make one perfectly.

'It is scientific,' said Peter Pumpkin Eater.

I looked at his fireplace. It was good but not showy like at The Ranch and the fire sometimes smoked and didn't get hot and big likes ours. Peter was better at growing things, like pumpkins. We called him Peter Pumpkin Eater because he had the best garden at Tralfamadore.

Mama's fireplace worked well. And to show how scientific it was, we'd show visitors how to open and close the flue, which was made from an old metal garbage bin lid. The most scientific thing was that Mama mixed cow poo into the cement mixture because she read in a book that the Indians did that. I don't know why or what kind of Indians. I don't think I was listening.

Every time we went to town, Mama collected cow poo from farm paddocks and put it into hessian bags left over from the bulk flour at the co-op. At least when the fire was burning, it didn't smell like cow poo.

'It's good for the garden too,' said Mama. Cow poo and blood and bone are the magic ingredients to make the garden grow strong. Cow poo doesn't really smell too bad but blood and bone makes you hold your nose it pongs so much. Mama said it's made from ground up bones and blood from animals. We couldn't be naughty because we might've ended up in the next batch.

We didn't really care about the garden too much. It was more fun to throw cow poo at each other than worry about how to make good fireplaces and grow veggies.

Now that we had a fire and most of the walls on our house, it was ready for us to sleep in. Mama made a room for our beds up high, like a stage – a *mezzanine*, said Mama. Our beds were lined up side-by-side and Mama slept underneath. It felt like a room inside a room and I wondered if this was what my hole in the wall was like in the farmhouse in Belgium. But I couldn't remember.

We celebrated with a fire in our new fireplace. The flames danced on all the walls while we ate stewed apricots with custard at our new kitchen table. We got the table from a farmhouse at Yowrie on the way home from town one week. It had pale yellow legs and a bare wood top. Strong and perfect.

'Imagine someone wanting to get rid of this,' said Mama, smoothing her hand over the scratches on the table top, her eyes sparkling. She soaked a rag in sesame oil and rubbed it into the timber. I think that might be scientific too.

New Age Philosophies

Mama went to India to visit a guru and each of us four kids went to stay with other people. It felt like years but was more likely three months. That was the normal amount of time that someone spent on a visit to a guru. I missed Billy, Couzie and Sara. Sara was with someone else in Sydney and the boys were at Tralfamadore with Rose.

Libby, the woman who looked after me in Sydney, was very tall. When I stood in front of her it was a long way up to see her face. Wherever we went I had to run to keep up with her. I missed Mama a lot and I was sad because Libby's son teased me all the time.

When Mama came home she was different, so beautiful. She always was but seemed more so now. We learned New Age Philosophies because Mama had found a guru of her own. She showed us a black and white photo of herself sitting next to him at his house in India. She wore a scarf around her head and looked like an Indian woman, her skirt touching the ground. We asked Mama how the guru managed to get through life with that long beard and big dress. Mama smiled fondly at the picture and tacked it to the back of the kitchen door. We felt his gentle eyes upon us when we toasted sesame seeds in the morning for breakfast.

Many of the things that Mama said now ended with *Nitya told me* ... His words were very important in our house and we listened to his wisdom through our mama.

Every day we ate lentils, chapattis and hummus and had to chew each mouthful of food one hundred-trillion times.

Mama came home from India with a beautiful silver urn. It wasn't made of silver but was smooth and shiny, dazzling you when the light hit it. We watched in amazement as she filled the urn with river water and balanced it on her head, just like an Indian woman. First you must fold a sarong into a small square and put it on your head. This is the pillow for the urn. Then you walk tall and hold the urn with one hand while balancing with the other arm. It's a much better way of carting water than carrying buckets where the handles cut into your fingers.

Mama was a goddess with her henna-dyed hair and tanned skin, bringing water up the hill in a silver urn. It sat on the fire and boiled water for our baths or to wash the dishes and clothes.

After Mama had been to India, Prem came to Tralfamadore and told everyone about his guru. This guru was called Bhagwan Shree Rajneesh. He had many rules: *wear orange clothes only; have a new name; wear a picture of me around your neck.* It wasn't long before other people from Tralfamadore went to Pune in India to visit this guru.

It was very bright in the bush after this, with everyone wearing orange. There must not have been any orange dye left at any of the shops in town. All over Tralfamadore, even The Ranch, there was orange flapping on washing lines or stretched out over the river rocks. When there was no water in the creek, everyone came down to the river to wash their clothes. It was orange for as far as you could see.

The bush school was behind our house, an outdoor

table with a makeshift roof. It now incorporated the rituals of the orange guru. The children learned yoga, dynamic meditation, and kundalini chants. We confused each other trying to relearn names. Gail became Vibuti, Eva became Garimo, Rose now Bhavana and Peter was Dinesh.

Later, Bhagwan told his followers that they could expand a little and wear other colours: purple, red, burgundy. So then the bush became other colours as the stocks of dye were bought for red, purple and burgundy. The only thing they couldn't change was the wood-beaded lanyard that had a photo of Bhagwan inside it. We noticed that Bhagwan, the orange guru, looked a lot like Mama's guru only his eyes were squintier.

With the New Age Philosophies came new ways of eating. I got pretty bored with lentils but I could eat chapatti bread forever. Chai tea is okay but it takes a lot of work to make, so Mama usually had bushman's tea. Mama liked to try new recipes. Sometimes they were good but other times I wished we just had spaghetti or rice.

'You will like this soup,' said Mama, ladling broth into our bowls. 'It's very good for you.'

We stared at the soup suspiciously: a milky broth with green leaves floating in it. We looked up at Mama.

'Stinging nettles. It's full of iron. The sting goes out of it when you cook it.'

Our skin itched.

'Eat it now!' demanded Mama.

We dipped our spoons, stirred them around until we felt

Mama's patience ending – a bit like the kettle just about to boil. So we brought the soup to our lips and slurped it warily.

Mama was angry at our gagging and threatened bed without dinner. When she realised that this usual threat had no effect, she snatched up a spoon and loaded her mouth. She swallowed.

We waited.

'Maybe Nitya is wrong about this one,' she said, and we exhaled slowly while she made us something else for dinner.

Strays

Our family had a habit of picking up strays: stray dogs, stray goats, stray chickens. Sometimes even humans. We were so proud of how much we could fit into our Holden that we took photos of it with a tank strapped to the roof and people hanging out the windows so we could remember it and laugh.

It's not certain if we didn't know how to tell the sex of a thing, or if we just weren't sexist but many of these strays had names that were gender opposed. We were especially proud of our one-egg-per-day layer, Bhagwan. She was certainly no guru but we considered her God-like and worth much more to the family living in the bush. Well, actually, she wasn't ours. She came to stay for a while from The Ranch and spent a lot of time squawking because a red fox was always prowling. We enjoyed the eggs that we got anyway.

Maybe we named these creatures before closer inspection, before checking the 'bits'. Discovering the 'bits' on Suzi didn't change our minds.

Suzy landed on our doorstep when we were staying at Cockatoo, near Melbourne – a black, curly haired dog that we reeled into our hearts. From the moment that he was booted out of a moving Vee-Dub on a lazy Saturday afternoon, Suzi became another one of our gang and was given bit parts in many of our extravaganzas.

Suzi was *off the back of a truck*, so to speak, just like many things that come our way from our grandfather, the panel beater. And such things held a special place in our hearts, like much of our childhood that had a cosmic feel to it, especially after the total eclipse of the sun.

The dog lived with us beside the sea, with the mean old milking goat that kicked Mama every day. This was before we moved inland to build the stone house above the river – our castle.

When Mama went to India on her spiritual journey, Suzi was sent out to someone on the coast and wasn't there when we came home. Some said that a dark man strangled him. Not a man with dark skin but a dark-thinking man. But Suzi could've been run over by a car or attacked by one of those enormous paralysis ticks that get dogs on the coast. Ticks love dogs on the coast. They burrow into the neck of the dog and suck on him until their bodies get fat and squishy. Then they let go of poison into the dog. The dog becomes paralysed. I hope that didn't happen to our Suzi.

The Flood

The black cockatoos gathered, screeching at each other. A shadow passed overhead as they flew above us, flashing red underneath their black wings.

Rain was coming; you could smell it in the air.

The wind rattled the corrugated iron roofing. The straight ghost gum at the back of the house swayed, dropping branches that made a whipping crack as they hit the ground. Relentless rain battered at the tin for hours. I chanted a mantra over and over, *Please stop raining, please stop raining.*

The rain continued and we battled to light the fire even with the use of kero – its blue-hued liquid fizzing against the damp kindling.

Endless hours became days. Wet, wet, wet. We watched the river. Held our breath. The water rose. Rose like a monster waking from slumber. Water covered the rocks and trees and crept steadily upwards.

Please stop raining, please stop raining.

I wondered if the water had ever covered our little hill. The water was so fast and strong. Trees sailed past, roots and all, some stopping at our crossing downstream and creating a new bridge for us, or a diving jetty – a new place to play.

If it stopped raining, the river would drain away into the sea in as many days as it came. If it didn't stop raining then we'd be stranded on our little island bound by the river on one side and the creek on the other. The only way out was along The Saddle out the back, a narrow ridge now made narrower by the rising waters on either side.

And if it didn't stop raining we'd run out of food because there is only so much to be picked from the garden in winter.

Please stop raining, please stop raining.

There was a meeting. I don't know how word got to us. There was always someone willing to travel around the bush regardless of the weather, regardless of the situation. In my mind's eye it was Maddy but I don't know for sure. The majority agreed that everyone should take what they can and head out to town.

We were adventurers on a quest carrying bundles of clothes on our backs. There were children, babies and dogs of all shapes and sizes. Some of us were good at being on an adventure. Others grizzled and wanted to be carried. It was a slow trek along the bush tracks, then out onto the road. Wet, slippery and muddy. The tears from heaven were finished so my need for chanting was over but the water was still rising as our convoy trudged along the rain-soaked earth.

At the first river crossing we assessed the situation. The roiling brown water was angry and thrashing at the riverbank on both sides. How would we cross even with the thick cable attached to a tree on both sides of the river?

The taller, stronger people took bundles and kids on their heads until we were all safely on the other side. It was a long day, this adventure, and we crossed four more rivers.

Mama said we could have hot chips at the co-op in Bermie but after a while the promise of that salty greasiness wasn't enough to keep us going. We didn't really care about it and just wanted to sleep.

It took all day to walk to the Yowrie Post Office where we kept our car. I fell asleep as soon as we got in it to drive from Yowrie to Bermagui.

The co-op was quiet by the time we got there – almost closing time. We took our chips to Alan's house up on the hill overlooking the sea. It wasn't raining there so we felt like we were in another country even though the river house was just over the mountain and down in the valley.

The chips did taste good though.

Dog Days

Mama went to Sydney to visit friends while we stayed with Moma and Popa in Caulfield, Melbourne. We liked this because we were fed goulash and noodles while sitting at a child-sized table, powder blue. Our sister, Sara, reigned supreme and we followed her orders without protest – mostly. We watched, star struck, when she played Scrabble with Moma. Their conversation seemed far removed from the bush and the longest words appeared under Sara's deft fingers.

Even though Moma and Popa were really only Sara's grandparents, we felt like they were all of ours. Popa and his brothers started a butcher shop when they came to Melbourne after the war. Popa was a judge back in Germany but they had to escape the Nazis. He couldn't be a judge in Australia so they opened the butcher shop and sold kosher meat.

Every time we saw Uncle Arnold, he'd hold up his hand with two missing fingers and tell us that he lost them picking his nose. Sara told us that wasn't true and he cut them off in the meat slicer. It made me a little nervous when Popa sliced the meat for goulash when we went to visit.

I was learning ballet and my class went to the Valhalla to perform *Snugglepot and Cuddlepie*. Moma, Popa and my sister were my chaperones.

For the performance, I was in the front row, dressed as a gumnut baby. The theatre was large and dark.

Monstrous.

The stage lights were so bright that I froze, mesmerised. I wondered if this is what the rabbits felt like in *Watership Down* when they had to cross the highway and got caught in the car headlights. I couldn't remember any of my steps as I swayed at the front of the stage while the rest of the gumnuts pranced around me.

The next week, when Mama came back to Melbourne, my ballet teacher suggested that maybe I didn't have what it took to be a dancer. I skipped out of the dance school on Nicholson Street to join the rough and tumble of my little brothers. Hanging out at the park at Curtain Square was much more fun than trying to point my toes, lift my chin and tuck in my tummy.

We jumped onto the whizzy-dizzy. Faster and faster, spurring each other on until we felt like chucking up all over ourselves. Yeah. Much more fun than wearing pink tights and tying my hair in a bun.

Mama brought something special back from Sydney for Sara for her birthday: a white fluffy puppy. Sara called him Cloud. He became another part of our gang and travelled with us in our battered Holden up and down the east coast.

Cloud came from a long line of pedigree, not born in Australia. His thick, white fur suffocated him in summer and he preferred the perfume of squished-up ants. When he got too smelly we soaped him up in the river, trying to tease the knots from his fur. He'd trot up the bank of the river, shake vigorously – he looked so funny with his fur flattened down – then turn to look at us before scurrying off to find an ants' nest to roll about in. He never smelled nice, no matter what we did.

He was our work dog, patiently standing guard at our blackberry tunnels, and pulling our red billycart up and down the hill.

Lofty, our grandpa, gave us that red billycart one Christmas. It was the best present we ever had. He made it from the bonnet of a red car in his smash repair shop. It had white stripes in a vee down the centre. The wheels had white rubber tyres with wire spokes and you steered with a rope that pulled the front wheels left or right.

Did he know how good this present was? Billy, Couzie and I squeezed into it together at the top of the road that went down to the creek. The road had a good curve to it and enough length to get some speed up before we hit the bottom where it leveled out.

Just before it leveled out, the three of us leaned to the right so that the whole cart toppled, leaving us in a pile of arms and legs, our bodies rippling with laughter.

We grabbed the rope and pulled the cart to the top of the hill. Repeated it over and over.

The billycart was also useful for carrying river stones up to the house. In this way, we helped Mama because before this we could only carry small rocks. The big ones looked much more impressive cast into the walls with cement-sand concrete that she made.

Mama wasn't always cementing rocks into the house. She was often in the garden planting veggies, wearing yellow rubber gloves. Mixing in the compost, planting new seedlings or taking out old, dead plants.

Sometimes Cloud kept her company, lying in the sun nearby or chasing skinks, big and small, through the garden while Mama weeded around the lemon tree.

The skinks were fun to chase when the grass was long after the spring rains and everything was bright green.

'Quick, Blaisy!' called Mama. 'Get the snakebite kit.'

I floated on the springtime air, oblivious to impending dangers until I realised that Mama was going to cut open our dog and suck out the venom of a redbelly black snake. The grass rustled beside me as the offender slithered away.

Without a vet for miles it was up to Mama to save our silly dog. She sucked out the poison and washed her mouth with salted water. We sat next to him for a long time, waiting, but he didn't get sick. He liked hanging out with us in the grass getting his white fur stroked.

Cloud carried on chasing skinks, as if he'd learned nothing. And we carried on as if nothing happened.

This was the way in Tralfamadore.

Elvis the Pig

The Mine Flat was named after an old mining shaft up the hill from the house. There was chicken wire around the gold mine because if you weren't concentrating you could fall feet first into the ground. Straight down. I think someone got stuck down there once for days.

Us kids peered over the edge. We didn't know how deep it was but an old car had been pushed into it and there was still room. We'd throw things down into the mine, giggling when there was a clang as we hit the old car. It was more of a tip now than a gold mine.

Someone told me that the Brassknocker Creek got its name around the same time as these mines were being dug for gold because the fossickers left stuff around. Maybe a doorknocker? Who knows what stories are true or not? Bush people love a good yarn and the more farfetched the better.

The Mine Flat was an open flat of land. Shree and Prem built a mud brick house and a sprawling garden. This all spread out below the old mine shaft and on a bend of the Brassknocker Creek.

The making of the mud bricks was an event. A gathering. People appeared out of the bush for a working party, a long production line of moulds and a stack of bricks left to set at the end of the day.

Us kids weren't impressed by the mudbrick making, or the building of the house, or the competition between the houses about who had the biggest and best garden. Although this garden was probably the winner on this side of the creek. Peter Pumpkin's was on the other side and his garden was the champion of all of Tralfamadore. We think he sprinkled magic dust over the plants at night.

Elvis the pig *was* impressive. He was enormous and his hair was black and stiff, like an old wire brush. He was as big as a pony! We were kept occupied by the question of how Elvis could fit into the ten-gallon drum that had been converted into a smoke house by Prem. We'd been told that smoked pig is good to eat but we were not really convinced by fancy stuff like that. About the most interesting meat we'd had was the Hungarian salami that Moma gave us when we went to Melbourne.

Apparently, smoked eel was pretty good too and we felt an affinity with them being smoked because we hated those wriggly things brushing against our legs when we swam in the river.

Elvis disappeared one day to the smoke house but we didn't bother to taste him. He'd be too tough and hairy for our liking.

Wart for Sale

Even though Alan had been here longer than us, he'd only now picked a spot for his house. He also lived at Bermagui so maybe he wasn't in a hurry to build a house.

It was very close to the edge of the river.

'Too close,' said Mama and we agreed.

It was the closest house to us and we could get there out along The Saddle and then by following the river upstream.

We'd leave our place, pass the tall spotty gum tree behind the house, walk along The Saddle single file and pass an old mangy wombat on the way. He'd be bumping into things in the daylight when he should've been in his burrow sleeping. There were lots of wombat holes along this track and I wondered if this was where *Wind in the Willows* came from – or at least the idea for it. Old mangy wombat reminded me of the blind mole.

The good thing about Alan's spot was that it was flat and easy to get to from the road. Everyone approved of this when the working party put in the uprights for the roof.

The road was awash with moonlight when we finished a day of work. The moon was so bright that we could walk along the road without a lantern. Richard (he was new to Tralfamadore) ducked and weaved along the road, talking loudly about everything in his funny English accent. He told jokes and we tumbled along the road full of laughter and silliness. A lot of the time we couldn't understand what he said but we laughed anyway. When we got home, we sat around the fire, sharing stories. The moon followed us everywhere.

I couldn't wear shoes because I had a giant wart on the end of my big toe. It didn't matter really because we didn't wear shoes much but I couldn't stop rubbing it.

'Want to sell me your wart?' asked Alan.

He smelled of beer and his eyes were always red and watery, like he'd been standing in front of the fire too much and had gotten smoke in them. There were tiny red lines like rivers inside the whites of his eyes. When he got close to me, my skin felt prickly, and I checked to see if I had ants running up and down my arms. His nose was red too and I tried to move away from him without him noticing.

'I can only do it by the full moon,' he said, waving at the sky.

I stared at the moon to see if it agreed with him but it just threw silvery beams at me. I wanted him to stop talking to me, so I agreed. He paid me five cents. I wasn't sure what I'd do with five cents since I didn't know when we were going into town again but I put it in my pocket and wondered how many mixed lollies it would buy at the top shop in Cobargo.

Alan kissed the coin and rubbed it over the wart and mumbled something. The wart on my big toe throbbed under the light of the shimmering moon and Alan looked happy with himself.

The next morning the wart was gone. I picked at my toe and searched everywhere for it.

'Where is it?' I asked Alan.

'It's mine now and you can't have it back,' he said. His eyes were squinty. I wanted him to prove that he had the wart. I could tell he knew where it was.

'It's mine alright. It's somewhere on my body that I can't show you,' he said and his eyes narrowed and he squeezed his lips together while I thought about it.

He pretended to look at some trees in the distance and rubbed his belly like he was full from breakfast.

I didn't ask any more questions and ran off to the river.

Garden Party

Don and Gail's house was upriver from Alan, closer to The Ranch. Don was keen to get the room built before Gail came back from town with their baby girl, Jasmine. She was out at Bega hospital, I guess, but who knows? Us kids weren't ever given details. She could have been in Melbourne for all I knew.

This was a proper room with four walls and a huge bunk bed. A mezzanine. Just about every house at Tralfamadore had a mezzanine. The bedroom walls were made from planks of wood and had windows and doors. Don, Gail and the three kids would be cosy in winter.

The rest of the house wasn't closed in like that. The walls were mud bricks with only three sides. I liked sitting at their big kitchen table because there was no wall in front of it so you could see out over the paddock. They were planning to plant lots of things out there. It was a big paddock.

Sometimes there were big red kangaroos out there. They'd stop, stand up straight, looking right at us, their pointy ears twitching from side to side. Then they'd lean over and push themselves off with their tail and bound away.

Between the house and the paddock was a forest of *tree of heaven*. It's a plant that came from China and it grew really fast. It was growing wild.

'Rampant,' said Mama.

Some people thought it was a pest and that no one should let it grow at Tralfamadore. If you got close to it, it was pretty stinky, so I agreed that it didn't belong there when we had tea tree and wattles that smell so good.

Below the forest was a gazebo, all set up for a garden party. The table was covered with fresh baked bread and hummus and custard pudding in the shape of a bunny rabbit. I looked at the bunny and thought of Fiver and Hazel escaping from humans. It was too perfect to eat and very special because it was set perfectly.

Somehow, they had running water that came down a gully from up the hill. This was heated by the oven so they had hot water all day long if they kept the fire going – better than taking buckets down to the river and heating it up every time you had to do the dishes. Also, there was a fridge. It ran on a bottle of gas and that meant they could have yogurt and cheese and it would last more than a day. That was how they made the custard bunny.

Visitors could stay in the little caravan parked up on the hill behind the house. Just like a hotel. It always felt like a hotel there. Don liked to drink sherry from little glasses and everything was organised. If you turned up at the right time, you might make happy hour.

In the bush, it didn't matter how good you made the house. The bush somehow got into things and took over. You couldn't keep anything out, like spiders or snakes or trees growing through the floor. The big brown snake we saw go behind the log in front of the house thought it was pretty good there too. Must have been after eggs or something.

Everyone freaked out. Kids jumped up and down. A dog barked. We could see the snake's head sticking out from the log. Did it really think we couldn't see it?

Don got the shovel from the garden and chopped its head clean off. It didn't stop moving though. We stepped back from the head in case it tried to bite us and waited for the sun to go down, until the snake stopped wriggling. Someone once told us that was what you have to do. Probably another far fetched bushwacker story.

Turning Feral

A pack of dogs was going crazy down at our swimming hole. Crazy-wild like nothing you could tell them would stop their racket. It had been happening a lot, packs of dogs rampaging through the bush.

It was talked about at tables and by the river. 'What should we do about those dogs? They've had the taste for blood. Turning feral.'

Us kids emerged from the blackberry tunnels and rushed down to the river to investigate. We made up our own little feral pack.

A dead kangaroo, fat and bloated, was wedged in a tree that overhung the waterhole. The stench stung our nostrils and the pack of dogs burst with hysteria.

'Will it explode?' asked Couzie.

Someone nudged the animal with a long stick but it didn't budge. Marco stepped out from the bank, left foot on a branch, right foot on the body – like a steppingstone. Us onlookers craned forward, waiting for the drama. The dogs were beyond excited now, saliva spraying sideways, teeth bared.

Marco rocked and nudged at the dead beast, the water rippling across the river. We held our noses dramatically; the pong made our eyes water.

The kangaroo came free, bobbing in the ripples and parting the branches of the tree. The dogs barked in trill tones – feverish – as the bulbous body floated down the Wadbilliga, the dogs following along the shore, carrying on like it might try to escape and bound away.

Boredom set in now that the excitement was gone, so we ran off to capture frogs. The dogs lost interest too and slinked away into the bush.

The occasional yelp or bark faded into nothing.

This small bit of excitement soon forgotten, we went back to the blackberries. From the break of day till the dusk of night, we were in the creek bed or in the blackberries. We scooted into the depths of the vines, prickly and dense, where we had carved out rooms and corridors just like in *Watership Down*. We sat in dug-out hollows sipping tea from a river stone or writing on a flat piece of slate using another powdery rock as a pen. There were so many colours: pink, mint green and white. My favourite made soft yellow words.

Our warrior dog, Cloud, stood guard. He was bored with our games and lay down to sleep. We'd hear a whine deep in the bush and Cloud would lift his head to listen, wary of those feral dogs in the distance.

The blackberries grew like a hedge around the bend in the creek and gave us bucket loads of fat, juicy blackberries every summer.

There was nothing like blackberry jam made with just-picked berries. Mama sometimes put too much sugar in the mix and the jam became toffee. It was so hard we couldn't even get it out of the pot. Then it burnt and turned the toffee black. The pot was no good now. We'd put it in the garden for the bush to claim.

When the jam worked well it didn't last. We ate it on chapatti bread cooked on the open fire. Warm and oozy. A jar of jam might've lasted a day or two. Maybe less if we didn't have to wait for the chapattis to cook.

Mama said that my daddy was coming to Tralfamadore. I didn't know what she was talking about. His name was Billy, just like my brother, and he was back in Australia after being in jail in France. Something bad happened there but I didn't know what. I was a little excited but also felt a bit strange because I didn't know what he was like. I didn't remember him. I knew his Mama, though, and she had big cow eyes and long eyelashes that looked even bigger through thick glasses. She lived in Melbourne.

Billy arrived on the back of a ute. A dog followed behind it, running along the road. Billy got out of the ute and had a huge smile like he was happy to see me. He was skinny like me and he had big eyes and long eyelashes like his Mama.

He carried a mandolin everywhere and everyone seemed to like him, even though they just met him. He smoked joints a lot and was happy. I liked him but I didn't feel sad when he left.

Markie

Markie came to live with us. He was very tall – maybe even twice as tall as Mama – with black hair. When he talked, I watched the freckle on his bottom lip dance. His smiles were small, like they were escaping, and he didn't tell stories like Mama. He told stories when he played guitar. I didn't understand them but they felt sad.

He didn't need to talk so much. I was like him. We liked to listen. When he walked he was never in a hurry. It made me feel peaceful. He was the best daddy we ever had but we didn't call him Daddy.

Once, he went back to Melbourne to make some music, and when he came back he had a huge water tank on the roof of the Holden. The tank was twice as wide as the car. We all laughed when we saw him through the trees, coming down the road like that. We asked him how he got past the police coming up the Princes Highway and he laughed too, his freckle dancing.

Pinned up on the walls of our house were some posters of birds that Markie brought back from the Royal Melbourne Zoo. With these, we learned the names of each kind that lived at Tralfamadore. I stared at the posters every day, trying to remember the names. I liked to hide under a blanket out the front of the house and spy on birds. My favourite was the willie wagtail. He was fast and cheeky but also pretty with dark, shiny feathers. I couldn't say the Latin words on the posters but I tried to match up their birdcalls with the descriptions next to each bird. The male eastern whip bird was the best because I could follow his sounds around the bush and I felt sad if his mate didn't answer him with her whip crack response.

Our favourite thing to do with Markie and Mama was paint rocks. We used rocks instead of paper because we didn't have much paper and it was more fun too. Markie painted a picture of Jesus with a donkey head on a cross. He and Mama had a long talk about Jesus and Jews and Christians that went on for days. I didn't understand any of it and I wondered why Jesus had a donkey head.

We were always making things. Painting rocks or writing stories or making songs. Everything that Mama made appeared to be made by magic. She wrote lots of stories and I wanted to be a writer like her one day. The first story that I wrote was about creatures that live in the clouds and turn on taps when we needed water. I think that idea came from *The Magic Faraway Tree* but actually I didn't know where ideas came from.

Markie helped Mama make our house better. He worked on all the things that Mama couldn't reach. He built a bedroom for Mama and him up behind the chimney – another mezzanine. It was the best place in the whole house, except if the fire was smoky. That just meant that you had to turn the garbage tin lid in the chimney to stop the smoke. When the room was finished we all asked why he made it Mama's size because his feet stuck out the end of the bed. He just laughed.

Markie moved the stable doors to the walls of this room so when you wanted to you could open all the doors and you felt like you were sleeping up in the sky. That was fine unless the possums decided to join you.

We went around the house collecting candle stubs – the ones that were too small to burn – and digging out the wicks before chucking them into an old pot we had on the stove. The wax melted into a smooth creamy mess. To this batch of wax we added lavender flowers so that the candles turned purple and smelled nice. We didn't have a lot of wax, so we made drippy candles instead of moulded ones. You cut the wick to the length you wanted, then dipped it into the warm wax. It was good to let it cool a little bit first so it wasn't too runny. Then, when the wax cooled totally, you dipped it again, let it dry and then repeated until the candle was thick enough to fit into the neck of an empty wine bottle.

When it was dark, Mama let us go around to all the candles and light them. It felt like we were at church all the time, especially with donkey Jesus looking down on us from his cross.

After dinner, we sat by the candles to draw or read. Watching the fire was nice but made you sleepy. Sometimes Mama would let me grind the coffee beans in her little wooden grinder. Even though I didn't like the taste of coffee, it smelled so good.

Mama said she used to make coffee like this when she lived in Belgium and was sitting down to do some writing: get out this little wooden grinder – it's from France – and put the cheeky coffee beans in the top through a hole (I called them cheeky because they looked like bum cheeks) then turn the handle with the red knob. It munched up the beans, making them powdery. When all the beans were ground up, open this little drawer and there's the coffee, all ready to use. This was when you put your nose up close to take a good sniff. Then warm up the milk and cook it with the coffee and sugar and put it in a bowl. It's like a soup coffee and Mama drank it a lot.

Instead of a mezzanine, we now had bunk beds that Markie built. It was almost like having my own room. I had a little shelf above my head where I could put a candle or my books. The last thing I'd do before going to sleep was to go into my bunk and read *The Faraway Tree*. I never knew what world those silly creatures were going to next.

Watermelon Pool

Jill and John were now called Samati and Mancha. Samati organised a working party at The Ranch to plant potatoes.

There were three big paddocks below the house where the potatoes were to be planted. Ben, the donkey, had ploughed the fields in preparation with Mancha guiding him in straight rows. There were lines and lines of grooves. I didn't like Ben too much, steered clear of him if I could because the one time that I rode him he turned around and bit me on the ankle.

Everyone had a turn at planting the potatoes. You needed special 'planting potatoes' – not just any kind. There were lots of big hessian bags full of them. I don't know why we needed to plant them when we already had bags and bags of them but I didn't say anything.

Cliffs surrounded The Ranch, as if a wall had been built around it to protect the place. It felt like someone was watching you. I didn't like to look up at the cliffs in case I saw someone watching me and sometimes I felt like my thoughts were not in my head, like someone else could hear them. I never really liked going to The Ranch because of this. It made me feel uncomfortable and I was happy to leave as soon as I could.

After planting, everyone went down to the Watermelon Pool to cool off. It was an expedition with bags of food; stuff to make tea, musical instruments and blankets to sit on. This meant that we'd stay on the sandy beach by the river for the rest of the day.

Just before the Watermelon Pool, there was a big open paddock that we called the Watermelon Flat. There were watermelon vines running across it, with tonnes of watermelons when it was the right season. It wasn't far to walk from The Ranch to this pool and we had to pass it on our way from home. Sometimes we'd stop for a swim and then keep going. And the best thing about the Watermelon Pool was that there was a giant rope attached to a tree where we swung from the beach out into the dark deep pool.

Billy was always climbing up the cliff on the other side of the beach at the Watermelon Pool. There was a rope over there too. The rope was so thick it was hard to grab hold of and burned your hands as you let go. It was worth it though, to swing from the rope into the middle of the river. It was so deep that you couldn't see the bottom. We'd always dare each other to let go over the deepest part. That's where the Lunka lived and it was a race to get back to the surface of the water before he grabbed your legs.

There were three best swimming holes at Tralfamadore: The Olympic Pool, The Watermelon Pool and the one at our place. I liked the one at our house best because you could see the rocks at the bottom and it wasn't too far to walk on a hot day. You could also lie on a lilo and float downstream all the way to the Olympic Pool. Problem with that was you had to carry the lilo all the way back.

There were lots of other good swimming spots on the river and the Brassknocker Creek but it depended on how dry the weather had been. Sometimes the creek had no running water and then you got covered in green slime. That was okay if you wanted to play slime monsters.

Jock

Jock didn't need to learn anything. He knew.

He sat up, ears alert, his intense eyes drilling me. This week he had decided that he was our dog. Chosen. We felt special. He had done the same at every other house at Tralfamadore and beyond, so that everyone claimed him. But he was his own master. Of course we had Cloud and we loved him but Jock was mysterious and unattainable. And very smart.

When you talked to Jock, he watched you with clever eyes. Bright blue. He understood. Everyone wanted him to be their dog but he would leave as if he had an appointment, then turn up unannounced, have a yarn (you did all the talking), chill out, then leave again.

Sometimes it was weeks until we saw him, other times months. Marco arrived one day with him in his ute, said he saw him on the Princes Highway up the coast towards Queensland. Hitchhiking. It was the return of a long-lost brother. We all thought that he was dead.

You could tell him to hop in the back of the car with a nod and he'd follow without hesitation. We wished he were our dog for real.

Blood and Bone

Markie brought mail from town. Mama was sad after reading a letter because her granny died. I couldn't really remember Granny Whitehead very well – only a little old lady with white hair. I knew that's not why she was called Whitehead. That's Mama's name from when she was born.

Mama walked down to the river to be by herself and have a good cry. That was the best thing to do when you were sad. She was sad because she loved her granny and her granny looked after her when her own mama was too busy. Granny Whitehead made Mama feel special when her own mama was mean to her.

This seemed to be the day for people dying because on the radio we heard that Elvis died sitting on the dunny doing a poo.

'Will Elvis be in the blood and bone now?' Couzie asked.

We tried not to laugh when he said things like this but it was hard because he was always saying something funny and then we got into trouble for showing off. It was good to see Mama laugh after crying about her granny. When she laughed her eyes crinkled up like mine.

Actually, Granny Whitehead didn't die the same day as Elvis. It took a while for the letter to come from Melbourne to the Cobargo post office, which meant that she probably died a few weeks before. Mama was sad about that too. She didn't get to say goodbye and she was being happy in the bush not even realising that her granny was gone.

To make us feel better, Markie made strawberry junket – my favourite. It took a long time to set but the kookaburras had just started laughing so hard I expected them to fall out of the trees. When they laughed like this we knew that it was only about ten minutes until it got dark and then we'd have dinner and the strawberry junket would be ready. You could set your clock by those birds.

Mama didn't seem as sad any more now that she'd had a good cry. I wanted to ask her if Granny Whitehead was going to be in the blood and bone like Elvis but I didn't know if she'd like the question. Only Couzie knew how to ask these things – maybe because he didn't think too long about them before he asked.

Peter Pumpkin Eater

I had to go to Peter Pumpkin Eater's house. He used to live in Sydney and he came to Tralfamadore about the same time as Anando and Bhavana.

You've never seen a bigger or better patch of strawberries in your life. Or bigger pumpkins. It was hard to stop calling him Peter Pumpkin Eater now that he had a Rajneesh name: Nehar.

So. I had to go to Nehar's house. By myself. I hadn't walked that far in the bush by myself before but was old enough now. I tucked my writing book under my arm and walked down the back of our house. My heart hopped in my chest and I tried to remember to breathe while following the narrow path along The Saddle, ducking branches and listening to the bush. I didn't know what I was scared of but walked faster in case something followed me. The insects buzzed in the treetops. I walked faster. Something dark loomed ahead but it was just the shadows under the trees. Silly me. I should be braver. Billy and Couzie wouldn't worry about this but had they done it all by themselves? I was walking fast now, almost running. The bush was talking to me. Is this what it was like for the bunnies in *Watership Down*? Did they feel like something was going to come out of the trees and eat them?

At the end of The Saddle I turned left and trotted down the hill – making sure not to touch the stinging nettles – to the school flat. There was no school there yet; that's why I was going to Nehar's house. The school flat was wide and open, it wasn't as scary here but snakes could still be lurking. I was brave. Almost there. I just had to get across the flat, down over the creek.

Crossing the creek took skill but luckily it wasn't too high, so I left my shoes on. The steppingstones were above water. Almost there. Just one more little creek and I could see the house. I cooeed. You should always cooee. This is the way at Tralfamadore.

I ran up the little hill, past the giant garden, to the house. Nehar and Garimo were waiting. I smiled, pretending that I always walked around the bush on my own, but I could still hear my heart pumping hard in my ears.

Nehar watched me bent over my writing. He thought about what to teach me that would set me apart from the younger kids. I knew this because I'd heard the adults talking about me and planning different things for me than the other children. I was the oldest now that Sara lived at boarding school in Melbourne.

Last week Bretski showed me how to bleed the brakes on Mama's old Land Rover. I wanted to learn to drive it but I couldn't even reach the pedals yet. Maybe when I'm ten.

'Today, we'll bake bread,' said Nehar.

He knew that I already knew how to bake bread but I went along with him. He could also tell that anything he taught me, I kinda knew too. There were so many things that they taught me that I'd been watching them do forever, so I knew what to do.

Eva … sorry, *Garimo* stood in the kitchen doorway, flour dusting her tanned arms. Nehar smiled at her as she brought ingredients to the table. I slid my book to the side and pushed my sleeves up my skinny arms.

'What do we need to make the bread rise?' he asked in his most teacherly tone.

I concentrated, my grey eyes crinkling into a big smile. 'Yeast,' I said, confident.

'Great!' said Nehar, and we watched the yeast bubble and froth in a glass dish like a wobbly monster.

'Hot or cool oven?' he asked.

'Hot,' I said, nodding at the sky.

'Yes! You're a quick learner,' said Nehar.

Outside, there was shouting. Someone running. Panting. My little brother, Billy.

On.

His.

Own.

'They need you,' said Garimo, muscly arms waving to Nehar.

The dough moved and shifted on the table as we rushed out the door to follow my little brother. We ran in convoy along The Saddle, past my house above the river, and followed Billy down to the swimming hole where all the kids and a couple of adults were standing over Anando.

Anando lay on her back on the rocks, bleeding from her head, the blood like the rapids downstream. *Anando looks peaceful*, I thought as I watched the bright red blood follow the curves of her face.

'What happened?' Nehar asked my little brother.

'She dived in head first,' he said, eyes wide, arms reaching out as if he couldn't contain the wonder of her doing that.

Nehar held up his hand. Shook his head. Then Billy stepped back, biting his lip as Nehar knelt beside Anando and balanced a bag on a large river stone. So much blood. He placed his hand on her shoulder and she opened her eyes. Smiled.

'I'm going to have to stitch you,' he said.

She nodded and closed her eyes while he rummaged around in his bag, muttering to himself, shaking his head at what was inside.

He held up a needle, squinted and threaded the eye with cotton. From his pocket he found a box of matches and heated the needle with a lit match, then offered her a sip of brandy from a tiny bottle.

He breathed in and steadied his hand and began to stitch her. The blood went thick and sticky and dark, Anando was quiet and brave.

I watched him, taking in every detail and smiling at my brother who was impatiently waiting to retell the complete gory episode.

looee

Mama jumped when she realised that Super Sullivan was here. 'He always sneaks up,' she said. 'He needs to learn to cooee.'

He was at our front door sitting high up on his big horse. His feet were wedged into the stirrups and the horse snorted and sprayed droplets over us as we craned our necks to get a good look at Super. He never got off his horse.

We always knew when Super had been around. Either his cows caused trouble or we'd see empty sardine cans nailed to trees. This was his way to make sure he could find his way back home to his cattle farm – better than leaving a trail of crumbs.

Mama was mad because one of Super's cows had eaten all the new plants in the garden and trampled the fence. It happened a lot but Super didn't seem to care. This made Mama angrier.

'This is private land,' said Mama. 'You should keep your cows on your own farm.'

Super looked down at her, and at my brother Billy. 'Sorry, love, that one got away. We're just passing through. Public land over there.' He waved his chubby arm towards the river and winked at Billy. 'Right girly?'

Billy frowned at Mama, then at me and then Couzie. We giggled and ran past Super on his big horse and down to the river, collecting Cloud on the way. Mama started telling Super what she really thought of him but we knew it wouldn't make a difference. In a few months the cows would be back on the riverbank.

'He needs to learn how to cooee,' said Billy, skimming a rock across the river.

'C-c-coo,' said Couzie, his hands either side of his mouth to make a trumpet. 'Right, Girlie?'

Billy punched Couzie and scowled.

'He's just not used to boys with long hair,' I said.

'Yeah, well, Marco says he's a creep,' said Billy.

'You don't even know what that means,' I said.

'Do so. Means he drools like Cloud does when he waits for us to feed him.'

'When did you see Super do that?'

'Last time he was here. I watched him watch Garimo in the river. I don't think those townies see each other in the nudie.'

'Supa the creep, supa the creeeep, supa, supa, supa,' said Couzie, wriggling his bum side to side.

I held my pointer finger to my lips and shushed my little brother, pulling him and Billy after me.

Super crossed the creek, going back downstream to his cows, with his stray on a loose rope. The cow munched lazily on grass. We followed them from a distance as the horse clopped across the creek, along the riverbank and then up the hill towards the Olympic Pool. We hung back because we knew where Super was going and we didn't want him to know we were following him.

At the top of the hill, he stayed on his horse (it's tail swishing side to side) amongst the trees that lined the beach area at the Olympic Pool. There was splashing and talking by the river and we could see bits of people through the trees. It sounded like a swimming race. Super watched for a long time as people swam up and down the pool and lay on the sand to dry off. Maddy and Marco were spurring someone on in the river. Garimo was there, her skin bronzed, blonde hair wet against her back. *Amazonian* is what Mama called her. We didn't know what that meant but she was so beautiful it was hard to stop looking at her. She came from Sweden or Czechoslovakia, or somewhere like that, and sometimes it was hard to understand what she said.

Super watched for ages so we went back to our own river hole and played in the water. Then we heard yelling: 'You dirty old bugger! Piss off will ya!'

There was lots of mooing and a few cracks of a whip, then the mooing faded. Super took his cows into the bush.

We collected as many flat skimming rocks as we could find, made three big stacks, and then had a competition to see how many jumps we could make in a skim and how far down or across the river we could get. Billy usually won. Couzie didn't like not winning but that's what happened when you were the littlest.

Super was the only person from town to ever come into Tralfamadore. One time we saw him at the Cobargo pub with a beer, standing around having a yarn with his townie mates. We had to look hard to make sure it was him because we only ever saw him on his horse and he had seemed like he was a giant. But at the pub he was about the same height as Mama, which meant he was more like a hobbit than a man.

Super and his mates watched us walk through the pub and whispered to each other, then laughed. We were used to that from the locals though. I reckon Super was more funny looking than us.

The only good thing about the Cobargo pub was the sarsaparilla and hot chips that Mama bought us. The carpet was sticky and there were lots of farmers standing around drinking beer and the telly was on showing the horse racing. We had to sit and be quiet – no showing off. That was a hard thing to do when you had a wriggly little brother like Couzie. It was better when we could get hot chips from the co-op in Bermie and run around on the beach, even if the gulls hassled us for a chip or two.

Granma Patsy

Granma Patsy and Lofty were coming to Tralfamadore from Melbourne. They had never been before. Mama said that Lofty was going to hire a van to drive up in. Lofty loved going bush but I don't know about Granma Patsy. I don't think she liked to get dirty or to sleep in a tent or anything like that.

When Mama was little they lived in a pub – her and Granma and Great Granma Scott and Aunty Beryl. Mama said it was lonely without brothers or sisters. I never got lonely with my brothers and Sara. Sometimes I liked to get away from them and hide under a blanket and spy on willie wagtails or go into the blackberry tunnels and read my books.

A white van ambled down the road. We heard it way before we could see it, even though it was much quieter than all the cars that ever came in here. It looked so shiny and new.

We ran down the hill to meet it at the river and to tell Lofty not to drive over the creek or he'd get stuck in the rocks.

Billy, Couzie, Sara and I were so excited to see Lofty and Granma. Granma saved something from her shopping every week, like a tin of beans or beetroot, and over the year it built up to a big box of goodies. It was like Christmas.

Granma got out of the van. She looked a bit frowny. I wanted to tell her not to pull that face in case the wind changed. Mama was always telling me not to pull faces but I didn't know what she meant since I felt like I mostly smiled.

Granma Patsy usually had a frowny face so maybe the wind changed when she was a little girl.

Lofty opened his door and we all ran to give him a hug. Lofty was never frowny and had to bend down low to reach us. He looked tired from all the driving, even though they didn't drive all the way from Melbourne in one day like we always did. They stayed in Bermagui in the hotel – that was only a couple of hours away. I don't think Granma liked Bermagui too much.

Lofty put out some camping chairs next to the van. We didn't need chairs with so many big rocks to sit on. Granma needed a smoke so she opened her special makeup case. Inside the case was an ashtray. We watched her having a smoke, which made her face even more frowny but she was happier after it.

Granma asked us why we weren't wearing any shoes. We looked at Mama for the answer. It was too scary to answer Granma's questions and we didn't know anyway so we didn't say anything. Then Granma looked like she had been sucking on a lemon.

Mama and Granma and Lofty caught up on all the news from Melbourne. After Granma had a few smokes, we all walked up to the house. I wanted to tell Granma that the shoes she had on weren't the best for walking around there but I didn't think she'd like me telling her that.

Lofty had a big box of stuff that they'd been collecting. There were lots of boring things like tinned food and packets of Deb powdered potato. We didn't need that with all the potatoes we planted at The Ranch. The best things were the jelly, lollies and the red cordial but we had to sit still and wait until they left before we could look properly at everything else. There were a few books, which was good. I was the only one who liked reading Enid Blyton so I got all of them but I'd read them out loud to Billy and Couzie later.

Birds of Australia

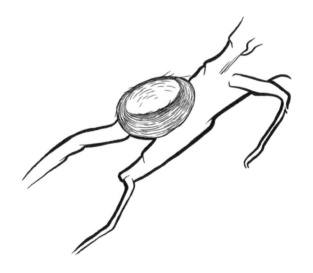

The bright rusty chest of a swallow flashed across the room, darted left then right. It picked up a twig from the floor and brought it back – pooping in full flight – to the nest on a cross beam above our heads. The bird twittered and flittered along the beam beneath the corrugated roof. Always busy. It went back and forth all day long.

It made me feel tired just watching it.

We checked our *Birds of Australia* poster from the zoo that was pinned to the wall with black tacks. *Welcome Swallow.* The nest took shape with mud and rubbish collected around the house, lined with soft white feathers. We took turns to sneak a look inside the nest for babies but all we saw were three small eggs. *Hirundo neoxena.* I tried to say the Latin words and copied them into my book. It said that the eggs take twenty-one days to hatch but I didn't know how long ago the eggs were laid.

We sat around the kitchen table, the candlelight flickering splashes of yellow light around the room. Mama was writing in a notebook. Long sentences in neat, curly writing. I wanted to know what her story was about but I didn't think I'd understand it. She was always writing in her book and I looked at the words and wondered how she made them look so beautiful.

The fire crackled and a log fell into the ash, the glowing embers throwing out tendrils of bright red and orange. Moths dived into the flames of the candles, which made the light flicker. Between the fire and the candles, light danced all around us.

Outside, the river talked to me, as did the creek, throwing up croaking frogs and the thump of a kangaroo as it bounded up the hill.

A high-pitched scream sliced the night. We sat stiff at the table, eyes straining in the soft light. My heart was like that thumping kangaroo. The night swarmed in. In my mind, I saw a dead woman, mouth ajar, the life draining from her.

'It's just a she-owl catching a rabbit,' said Mama, without looking up from her writing.

I tried to rearrange the image in my head. All I could manage was a frightened little Fiver in the claws of a ravenous owl as he was swallowed up by the darkness. Going to sleep was hard when you couldn't turn off these pictures.

In the morning, I rushed to the *Australian Book of Birds.* There was nothing under *she-owl.* But under 'Owls' there was the description of the sound they made under Barking Owl as *wavering human scream.* My skin prickled and I saw the dead woman lying in the creek, then Fiver with blood matted on his downy soft fur.

The drawing of the owl didn't look frightening. It had beautiful patterns on its feathers but that hideous sound was hard to explain. I tried to scrub away the picture of Fiver in my head by looking up willie wagtails. They were so naughty that I had to smile.

I needed to go to the toilet down in the garden. It was dewy outside. I was sitting on the step next to the fireplace, putting on my gumboots, and there was something small and grey on the floor. A tiny bird! Its teeny eyes were closed and looked like little crosses. It was wrinkled and ugly. I looked up at the nest. That was a long way for a little bird to fall.

Carefully, I picked up the shrivelled creature and took it, *her*, out into the garden and buried her under the lemon tree. I made a cross out of two twigs – they reminded me of her eyes – and told her that she was safe now. I hoped that her mama and daddy wouldn't be grumpy with me for taking her away but I couldn't leave her on the ground to get squished by our gumboots when we made our porridge.

Cloud came sniffing and sat quietly next to me. I knew he understood what I was doing. We didn't need to talk to tell each other stories. I bent over and wrapped my arms around his neck and he licked me. He smelled pretty bad from rolling around in ant nests and his white fur was matted in clumps. He had squinty eyes that reminded me of Mama's guru.

I tried to imagine him living in the snow, where he came from, but I'd never seen snow except in *The Lord of the Rings* and even that was inside my brain, not a picture. I tried to recall the description in the book, the snow part, but then I really needed to do a wee. While I did a wee, I remembered that we lived in the snow in Belgium but I couldn't picture that either, even if I squeezed my eyes tight to try to bring the memory back.

I got off the toilet and threw a cup of ash onto the pile. Markie would have to dig another hole soon because it was getting full. I put the lid on with a rock on top so the wind didn't blow it open and attract the goannas.

Screetch! Something down at the river. I tried to run but my gumboots were too big and they rubbed my bare feet.

'Blaisy, look at this!' Billy was down the creek checking on the frogs. When I got to the top of the hill above the creek, Billy put a finger over his lips: *Shhhh.*

I looked at the big tree he was looking at and halfway up was a huge goanna with a bunny in its mouth. The goanna and the rabbit were very still. Then the goanna swallowed the bunny in one go.

'Wow! Did you see that?' asked Billy, his mouth a big O. We couldn't wait to race up to the house to tell everyone what we saw. I think the goanna in the story was bigger than in real life and the bunny screamed louder too. But like Mama says, *Don't let the truth get in the way of a good story,* and she had lots of good stories.

After breakfast, we wanted to play in the blackberry tunnels but Mama said it was time to get cleaned up. 'We're going to town.'

'Can we get sarsaparilla?' asked Couzie.

Mama didn't answer. Squinting at the fire because it was blowing smoke into her face, she boiled water for a bath using the silver urn. I thought about when she told me not to pull faces in case the wind changed but I wouldn't dare say anything. It was not a good idea to be a smarty-pants. Couzie said lots of things that came into his head, so he'd get a smack. Sometimes we all got a smack just because she didn't know who was naughty or who was showing off. Showing off was just about the worst thing you could do.

Turned out that when we got to town we just kept going all the way back to Melbourne.

Past Bega.

Past Merimbula.

Past Eden.

Stopped at Lakes Entrance for hot chips with salt and vinegar.

Counting the white lines down the middle of the road until we fell asleep and Mama carried us into the house at Canning Street. The house that waited for us while we played in the river all day long.

There were other people living in the house too but we had one room to sleep in. While we were in Melbourne we went to Lee Street Primary School. It was a straight line down Canning Street, towards the city, past Mr Zable's house, then the man who polishes his car every day, then Curtain Square. Sometimes, we'd see Mr Zable with his suitcases coming home from Victoria Market. I didn't know what was in those cases. Maybe he was a secret agent. He was always very smiley though, so maybe he was a smiling assassin like in those James Bond movies.

On my first day at Lee Street Primary School, I burnt myself heating up milk for my breaky. You should've seen the huge blisters I had on my chest – they were so cool that I showed them at show and tell on Monday morning. The nurses at the Royal Children's Hospital had wrapped lots of white bandages around me and I felt like a mummy. I hadn't been to school before, except for kinder for a few weeks.

The only person I knew was Carlos who lived a few houses away from us in Canning Street. His dad had lots of lemons growing in his front yard and his older brother had a car that was very special; he polished it all the time.

Carlos was older than me, so I don't know why he was in grade one. I was a little scared of him because when we passed him and his friends they would do rude things with their elbows and say *va fungula*. I didn't know what it meant but it couldn't be nice.

But Carlos wasn't with his friends at school and the teacher asked him to help me with my reader. He sat with me and was very friendly and nice and taught me to read. I could already read but I did learn some new words from him and the teacher was very happy.

On the way home from school we passed Curtain Square so we had to stop to have a go on the whizzy-dizzy. It was time to go home when we all wanted to have a good chuck up.

We didn't stay long at Lee Street Primary School. Just as well because the other kids thought we were weird with our egg jaffles for lunch and I never knew the words to all the Abba songs that the other girls danced along to in the playground.

Water Child

We giggled over a cup full of chickpeas, their little beaks chirping to each other as we covered their heads with water to soak overnight.

The next morning, we boiled them and watched the broth go frothy and create a scum on the surface. The pot was poured over the strainer, steam escaping with a hiss. We added paprika, tahini and lemon juice, then killed it with the masher. We mashed it and smashed it until it was thick and creamy, then scooped it up with chapatti bread cooked over the outdoor fire.

We didn't hang around. Ate and ran. Long enough to get flour up our arms and under our fingernails. Long enough to smear burnt crust on our lips and to lick the creamy paste from our chins. No hello or goodbye. No left overs for Cloud or Bhagwan the chook.

We left Mama with her rubber gloves on, mixing cement, and Markie banging nails into something. We raced down the hill to the creek and got back to damming it up, building bridges and fortresses and pools for our captives – little brown frogs. The sun glinted off our brown bodies.

There wasn't always water in the creek. Every year was different. When it flooded, the creek filled with clear, sweet water. When it dried up, bright green slime collected at the edges. We gathered the slime with sticks and draped it over our bodies, becoming slime monsters.

As summer came, the slime dried out and became white chalky marks draping the rocks. We knew the creek was still there because it talked to us from far below, teasing, hiding. The frogs went into hiding too, or moved down to the river.

The river always talked to me. Her voice was very slow, enchanting and swirled around me. I couldn't escape her. She told me stories about the bush. Old stories that I didn't understand. But mostly she told me how good and perfect I am, about the adventures that I will have, how everything will be okay. She answered questions that I hadn't asked and my heart filled up and up as if the water was flowing into me. The river told me that I was her child and I will never need more than I have right now and that she will look after me.

Did Mama know this? I felt like I had water running through me and over me and when we swam in the river I was made new over and over again.

Every time I felt sad or scared, I floated to the river in my head and the feelings went away. I wondered if everyone else at Tralfamadore felt like this but I didn't know how to ask.

School House

Tralfamadore needed a school. It had been decided. Everyone had different skills to teach the kids.

The tractor was brought out to clear a space – a big open paddock that we called The School Flat. Above The School Flat was another spot made for the school. As always, afterwards there was a bonfire and lots of music.

The school had a dirt floor, upright poles and a roof. It was a start. My monkey brain imagined us lined up at tables like in *Little House on the Prairie.* A blackboard might be out the front. I couldn't wait to learn things and to write them in my book. Every time we walked past the house on the way to Nehar's place, I imagined our rows of tables and all the books that I'd be able to read. My heart longed for it.

People came and went, travelled to India. They were going to see the squinty-eyed guru. Sometimes they were gone for months, sometimes only weeks – it depended on how much money they had. When they came back they waited to save up dole money to go back again or they went to Canberra to work and save as much as they could.

The schoolhouse didn't change. We planted crops of corn, then tomatoes on the school flat. People came back from India and taught us kundalini meditation, all of us lined up, standing on sarongs on the school flat. Or we'd listen to Bhagwan speaking on a tape recorder if we had batteries for it. Everyone nodded their heads at everything he said but I didn't understand a word of it. Or we'd harvest the corn, mostly eating it before it was ripe because it was sweet and juicy like that.

Mama wrote to the New South Wales board of education and we got special lessons sent to us in envelopes. We did our learning in the morning and then went down to the river until she called us back to eat. There was no time to get hungry when you were busy building fortresses and tunnels or dive-bombing into the river.

The schoolhouse never held any lessons under that roof because everyone was busy going to India. Bretski and Bhavana moved into it after a while, so I gave up on the idea of a blackboard and desk.

Monkey Time

We still had our house at Cockatoo and we went to Cockatoo Primary School for a few months. It could have been months or maybe only weeks. My teacher was Mr Stroud and I listened to everything that he said while most of the other kids fidgeted and mucked around. My best friend was Wendy James and we thought it was funny that her brother had two first names: David James. They lived in the house below us on the hill at Salisbury Avenue and we'd visit each other through gates that joined our properties. Wendy was in grade four with me and we traded swap cards with little girls on them.

There was a boy who liked stroking my arm. He'd always sit close to me and smile. I liked him too but we never played together at lunch time. There was also a girl with beautiful, thick brown hair who had to have it all cut off because she kept getting nits. I didn't know what nits were before then. Other kids said it was because she was dirty and didn't have baths but I didn't have baths much in the bush and I never had nits.

Every school day my brothers and I walked down the steep Hillside Road to Pakenham Road and followed Cockatoo creek before cutting through some paddocks to get to Cockatoo Primary School.

We didn't see Markie much any more. He moved back to Melbourne. Billy and Couzie hid in a giant wicker basket because they weren't very happy when Markie left for the last time. He was the best daddy we ever had.

He gave me a big monkey that was flat with a long tail. I called it Pancake and treasured it for years. It stayed at Tralfamadore all the time and eventually got eaten by bush mice, like anything else that was left there.

Our family was shrinking now that Markie was gone and Sara was at boarding school. Also, someone poisoned Cloud with a piece of steak with ground up glass in it. Mama had to get his body out from under the house at Cockatoo so that we could bury him. Seems like everyone was leaving, then Wendy said her family were going to live in Queensland because the weather was better up there. I'd never been to Queensland so I couldn't compare.

It didn't matter, really, because I still had Mama and Billy and Couzie. We went back to Tralfamadore after a while and there were lots of people to talk to and time to swim in the river.

Birth Day

The radio balanced on the sawn-off log and I leaned in to fiddle with the knobs. Mama was down in the garden cutting back the asparagus, which had started to seed. In the house, my brothers wrestled over something unknown even to them. I held my breath as I searched for the channel on the radio. Turning the nob one way then the other. The radio cracking and whistling. Finally there it was, the BBC channel. I hoped that I hadn't missed that week's episode.

The deep voice of an English man began reading an episode of *Watership Down*. I could feel the anticipation in my tummy. I wished I could listen to the stories all day long but I had to wait and sometimes I couldn't tell what day it was because I didn't have a way of finding out.

I didn't know that you could make up a story that was so real. It felt like I was inside the story. They were my friends.

Mama called me from the house. 'We're going to the Toucan Club!' she said as she separated Billy and Couzie with a look. The Look.

We took the road way to the Toucan Club, which is the last house on Tralfamadore, or the first house if you arrive from town coming by the Wandello fire trail. We walked this way from our house – rather than the creek – because we were carrying things that Mama needed and it was easier. It was boring though because it meant we couldn't stop at the School Flat or Peter Pumpkin's House, or the Sugar Shack or The Mine Flat because they were off the road. Mama was in a hurry.

Once we got to the Toucan Club, my brothers and I ran

down to the creek to see the other kids because grown-ups are boring. We were in the water before we even said hello.

Puffy clouds swam across the blue sky as I lay on the smooth rocks edging the creek, thinking about the total eclipse of the sun the other day. The radio warned us not to look at it because it would burn our eyes. I couldn't resist.

The sky went grey that day and the birds stopped chirping. The birds were quiet now, but it was because of the heat. My eyes still worked fine and I wondered who 'they' are on the radio and if they can be trusted.

The rocks were burning my bum, so I got up to see what the others were doing. Billy and Lucy were squatting by the creek prodding little frogs. Billy's skin was dusty brown from the sun, and his dark hair was matted at the back. In the water stood our brother Couzie, showing off. He hurled the biggest rock he could lift, which went *kerplunk* in the clear water. We tried to count the ripples, but got distracted when Tao came crashing into the pool from a rope tied to a river gum.

An enormous March fly annoyed me (and it wasn't even March) so I grabbed a tree-branch-fly-swat to whack it. The sting lingered. Revenge was diverted to hunger when my tummy rumbled. I grabbed my skirt to use as a bag and trotted off, promising the others food.

The house was busy. Suzy boiled water, Gail made chai tea. Maddy was strumming his guitar, humming softly.

'The baby's coming!' someone said, excitedly. Now I knew why Puj had been hurrying to finish building the bed.

It had stood impressively for a week or two in the room with nothing else but a single chair.

In the end room loomed the birthing bed. Helpers gathered. Mama was squeezing Anando's hand, whispering in her ear. Encouragement. Since Mama had four kids, she knew stuff. Puj sponged Anando's forehead. Her wild brown hair was flat and wet against her neck. Wafts of Patchouli tickled my nose. The sun tried to get in on the act, sending green and blue shards of light through the glass bottle ends that were cast in the rock walls.

It was quiet except for a low rumble coming from Anando's tummy. I wasn't sure how a baby could fit in there, though I felt it kick a few days before. The noise was growing longer and deeper. My eyes widened and I thought maybe the baby was coming out of Anando's mouth but I was sure that the baby came out the other end. It wasn't long ago that I'd seen the goat have a kid – you know, a baby goat – and it almost fell out, all slippery and wet.

I stood behind Mama to hide my fear. The look on Anando's face wasn't good; it was all screwed up, like she might need to do a poo. Then I realised that the sound of an angry animal was coming from Anando. She sounded like a man. Or some wild animal. I looked at each face leaning over the bed. No one was scared, just smiling and whispering and cooing. Anando seemed to be somewhere else.

After a while I got a bit sick of it. Nothing happened. How long does it take to have a baby?

'There's the head!' said someone, making me jump.

I saw a big mound between Anando's legs and everyone rushed to the end of the bed. Not long after that, out fell Basil Bracken Toucan Smith, all slippery and wet.

The baby boy cried and everyone was busy cleaning up so pretty soon my curiosity was gone. I remembered my rumbling hunger. I grabbed nuts, dried fruit, chapatti bread and hummus.

I delivered a picnic to the others by the creek who feigned death by hunger and disgust at having to wait so long for my return. Their whining turned into white noise because in the short skip back to the creek, I felt bigger. I told them about the baby but they didn't seem interested. We stayed away from babies as much as possible.

Peace and Love

We went back to Melbourne again. We had to go to school for a while to make the education people happy. This time we went to Princes Hill Primary School. I was going to be in grade five.

The teacher asked me a few things and decided that I should be in grade six. It didn't really matter to me; I was excited to make some new friends. Only problem was that most of the kids called us crazy hippies but lucky we were good at things and they liked to play with us. My favourite game was knuckles and I hung out with Jenny. Jenny was going to high school in America the next year. That seemed like a long way to go for school. I didn't know where I was going. Maybe somewhere in Bega.

Mr Street, the grade six teacher, liked my projects. I liked them too. I spent a long time working on my Australian History project about Eureka and I got an A plus. I liked school. Well, I liked making projects and learning about photography; you could keep the maths.

We were at the Carlton baths, down Rathdowne Street and across the road from the council flats. It was pretty hot and just about everyone from Carlton must have been there on this day. Mama let us come by ourselves, so long as we stuck together. I was hanging out with Jenny. Billy and Couzie were there with some other kids from Canning Street. Couzie was showing off. Again. Mouthing off. Lucky Mama wasn't there or we'd all be in trouble.

On the other side of the pool was a group of Lebanese kids from the flats. They were looking pretty frowny.

Couzie waggled his bum at them and they were standing up and walking around the edge of the pool. Couzie laughed at them. Then he ran out the glass doors onto Rathdowne Street. He was pretty fast for a little kid but it was easy to spot him with his white hair.

The Lebanese boys were looking at us now and pointing at Billy. 'Oi, you. Stinky hippy. Your little brother is gonna get it next time. But now, you're gonna get it!'

Billy, Jenny and I ran quick as we could out and up Rathdowne Street. We were pretty fast too, especially with twenty kids chasing us. There was no time to stop at Tony's fish n chip shop like we usually did. We just breathed in deeply, smelt the chips frying, as we ran past the door.

When we got to our street, Benny Zable was leaning against his combi wearing a bright singlet with a peace sign on it, talking to Mama. His dark curls bounced while he talked. He tried to keep his curls under control with a rainbow headband but it didn't work. I was in love with Benny and wanted to be an activist like him when I grew up and drive around in a brightly painted combi just like his.

Mama was loading up the four-wheel drive with food and blankets and stuff. We were leaving early in the morning, probably four am, to head back to Tralfamadore. I was happy about that. The river was so much better than stinky chlorine and we could stay clear of those Lebanese kids for a while.

Eleventh Summer

We were wild children dancing with the waves by the deserted beach, the sun catching the tops of our heads as we bobbed in the foamy bath. Nearby, other children clamoured over the rocks, prying oysters from their sleepy lives, chucking them into a bucket already brimming with grey gnarly shells. With the bucket tipping and swaying, the children skipped and hollered back to camp.

'Hey, guys, come get some. Quick!'

'Yeah, hurry or we'll eat 'em all up.'

Our camp stretched out below salty trees and washing flapped in a stiff breeze. The fire spluttered and popped as the billy burped with boiling water. A log, our kitchen seat, held one small child still in nappies. His tummy was fat and his arms skinny, his hair crazy from the wind, the sand, and the salt. Surrounding him was a messy group of ancient army tents, creaking and old. We raced up the beach full of bravado – whistling and shrieking with mammoth tales of daring.

Four brothers clamoured for a spot on the log. Lined up they looked like Russian dolls – smaller versions of each other with squinting eyes. None had seen a brush or bath or a pair of shoes in a good while – hair taking on a life of its own. Everyone claimed extreme fainting hunger, the competition escalating.

The oysters were spirited from their shells, hardly seeing the light of day as they were slurped from their homes into the mouths of squawking baby birds. Not by me; oysters slide down your throat like large lumps of snot. *Argh!*

The faithful Labrador waited patiently for handouts, which didn't appear, except from the one in nappies. With food in their bellies, the boys challenged each other and were off over the sand dunes, their voices trailing in the wind, the dog hot at their heels, the one in nappies toddling in their wake.

I loved the boys but sometimes they gave me the shits, laughing at me when I had sand in my bum crack. The boys were good value but noisy; the oldest was Roland (a bit younger than me, we called him Worm), then Billy, then Vincent, then little Johnnie (still in nappies). Then there were my little brothers: Billy and Couzie.

I ignored the boys calling me as they waved and shouted some story at me from the rocks. I was busy, with my plaits. I wandered around the campsite holding tightly to one finished plait, looking for a tie. I found Johnnie, dad to the boys, squinting into the camp oven. His eyes watered as he tried to shield them from the smoke.

'Hey, Johnnie, do you have a lacker band?'

'Eh?'

He looked at me as if I were an alien. He rummaged through tin plates, muttering to himself.

'There you are, little miss pig-tails …'

'Thanks, Johnnie. Hey, they're plaits, ya know?'

'Hmm … oh, okay, Miss … Plaits.'

He retrieved his bread from the fire, swearing at the hissing billy teetering over the flames.

The lacker band did the job although it pulled a couple of hairs and made my eyes sting. Rubbing them made it worse, on account of the salt and sand. I hung around long enough to see a blue kombi pull up and a family tumble out. I didn't linger, since there were babies, and they were bad news because before you knew it, you were stuck looking after them. Then, you had to listen to adult conversation. I'd heard all the stories a trillion times plus infinity, especially the ones from Mama.

I picked up a piece of Johnnie's warm fresh bread, dipped it in honey, and raced over the sand, which grated my toes but felt good.

I undressed on the bank and swam the inlet, heading for the rocks, the choppy water frothing around my ears. I imagined myself a beautiful mermaid, with my hair in long plaits, adorned with a garland of seaweed until I remembered that there were eels in the water. The boys were impressed that I no longer needed the rubber tube to help me cross, like last summer.

'Come on, Sis, hurry up!'

'Come see these giant crabs; they're real fast.'

'Fast as lightning!'

'They're grouse and real snappy.'

Worm and Billy cackled, clamouring over the rocks, poking and prodding at nooks and crannies.

The novelty of crabs wore off when we had scared them all into hiding, so we sat on the rough rocks, the spiky bits sticking into our bum cheeks, with our feet in the little warm pools of water, nudging at periwinkles with our toes. The oyster bucket stayed empty, and only the promise of food got us back across the inlet, to the camp, when so many grown-ups were around.

By the late afternoon, the camp had swelled with people as they set up more tents. They'd come to Bermagui from up and down the coast, even Melbourne and Sydney. The whole place was warming up to it: the dance at Murrah Hall. Kids were running everywhere and you couldn't really tell who belonged to who. Before we knew it, we were getting our faces washed and our hair smoothed, with little lasting effect. Mama even found me a skirt. It was made from red woven hemp and had blue flowers embroidered on it. I unplaited my hair and liked how it had gone all kinky, like the waves.

Later, at the hall, the band was setting up. Maddy was holding a cigarette with his teeth while he tuned his guitar, *twang, twang, twang* ... Margo, the back-up singer, was counting into the microphone, *One two, one two* ...

Children ducked and weaved through the crowd. Before long, the music was turned up. Up to my earlobes and out through my hair. I was in heaven. I danced, I jigged, I rocked and I waved. I made my skirt billow out around my knees and I danced with Worm until my bare feet hurt.

'Hey, look at this,' said Worm.

I gazed into the eyes of my stomping partner and felt strange feelings like never before. The moon was high and I felt even higher, from the beating of my feet on the wooden planks to the twirling and the whizzing of my new skirt.

It was strange when the band stopped for a break and a drink at the bar. I couldn't stop the buzzing feeling at the end of my toes and my fingertips and even along my hair, which seemed even kinkier than before. I went outside to find my brothers – were they full to their eyeballs with this feeling?

Tommie, from the band, was sitting on the back steps rolling a cigarette. He shifted his weight onto his elbows to lean back and look at the sky. My brothers were now forgotten as I skipped towards Tommie, who I secretly wanted to marry. I smiled from ear to ear. All the kids thought that Tommie was IT. He was old enough to drink and smoke and drive a car, but he still talked to us as though we were real people, rather than little kids. I ran up the steps and plonked down next to Tommie and pulled my knees up to my chin and wrapped my arms around them. This was mostly to still my jiggling muscles that were still dancing.

'There's my girl. How are ya, mate?'

Tommie grinned and put his arm around me; this made me tilt my head towards him. I was still bursting with this love of the music. I could smell the tobacco smoke in his clothes and a hint of beer on his breath. I closed my eyes to the world in an effort to trap it all, but the darkness made me a little dizzy.

'How's that music, baby? Gets the place really jumpin', doesn't it?'

Tommie's deep velvety voice was mesmerising, but I could barely hear what he said with the music still echoing in my ears, so I stayed with my head on his shoulder, eyes closed, and sighed.

'Do ya like it?'

'Yeah, Tommie, I really, really love it. You're a great bass player.'

'Thanks, princess; it's all I live for.'

'It's like a whole other planet.'

Tommie laughed.

'Hey, baby, have you ever kissed someone?'

'Course I have, Tommie. I kiss me brothers and Mama and everyone else, all the time.'

'No, I mean kissed like a grown up?'

'Nah, I'm not a grown up.'

'You are, just 'bout.'

'Nah ...'

My eyes closed.

Then I felt something warm near my ear and shrugged it away before realising that Tommie was kissing my neck. All the wild and wonderful feelings turned to a strange spasm in my guts, my belly, and even though I didn't know why, I knew I no longer wanted to marry him. I was sure I didn't even like him now that I was so close to his face. My tummy flipped and I suddenly understood what Mama meant when she said to listen to your gut feeling. Funny how you don't know the real meaning of something 'til it's right in your face.

He put his tongue in my ear. The feeling was icky, wet and warm, and my knee went into his chin with a cracking sound. I'm not sure, but maybe he bit his tongue 'cos he swore real loudly.

I ran back into the hall and almost crashed into Worm. The music came booming out of the amps, and he grabbed for my hands before I could say no. That music! I felt dizzy and happy. Worm's hair stood out all around his head like a crazy halo, and his stomping rhythm seemed all out of whack, but the smile on his face was like the sun. I was so happy that I felt like I was flying across the sky with the moon and the stars. I flew and flew until my legs were numb.

The moon slowly dipped behind the trees. The party slowed and was now just a low hum. Me, Worm and the rest of the boys piled in with the other kids. We didn't care about the babies, who were sound asleep and just a jumble of arms and legs inside the blue kombi van.

I dreamed of beautiful mermaids dancing in the waves, wearing periwinkles in their blonde hair, which radiated from them like rays of moonlight. They threw back their heads and laughed at length, exposing pale throats. The stars glittered on the surface of the water, winking at me, as the mermaids swam the inlet and raced each other to the rocks and back until they lay exhausted on the sand. They sat up when they heard voices approaching and grew human legs that carried them swiftly across the sand dunes and out of sight, leaving a trail of faint giggles and the soft splashing sounds as they returned to the deep sea.

Enid Blyton Has a Lot to Answer For

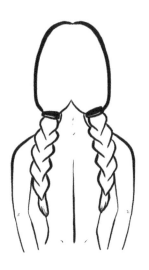

Over the long hot summer I dreamed of secret societies and clubs and new girlfriends. I read and reread my handful of books while I cooled my toes in the river. Mama said that next year I would be going to boarding school because she didn't know enough to teach me any more.

Back in Melbourne I packed a bag that would take me to another life where shoes were mandatory and I had to brush my hair every day. Not just brush it but actually wear it up in a ponytail or plait. Lucky I was good with plaits.

On my first day at boarding school, I stood in the doorway of the room that was dominated by four single beds. Two heads lifted as I entered and I walked straight for the empty bed under the window. I couldn't understand why this one hadn't been taken.

That night, I learned why. The windows of the hundred-year-old building shook and rattled. The ghost of Nelly Fitchett wandered the corridors at night while young girls from all over the globe shared ghost stories in their darkened rooms. Shadows passed by our room, showing through the strip of light under the door and the wind moaned in the tower. This tower was home to Nelly who, according to legend, swan-dived from its window to a splattered death on the concrete three stories below. The real story was that she died from meningitis. As Mama would say, *Don't let the truth get in the way of a good story.*

I'm not sure what I expected from this adventure. After reading every single Enid Blyton book, I thought it would be something different but it wasn't all bad. One hundred girls gathered in the dining room at six pm. It was dinner time. Or 'tea' time as someone called it, though I saw no sign of tea. We stood obediently behind our chairs, heads bowed while someone, a 'mistress', said grace. I tried not to stand out in the crowd.

Each table took turns to line up for the buffet food. Curried shrimp in vol-au-vents. I don't think I had ever had curried shrimp before and it tasted pretty yuk. After *tea* my tummy felt off and I had to hug the toilet for most of the night. I didn't want to ever eat curried shrimp again.

At seven, the clamouring of a bell woke me through a croaky loudspeaker demanding that we rise and start our day at the Methodist Ladies College. I couldn't say that this was better than being woken up by kookaburras.

It was a routine that I repeated for six years.

I kissed a boy in year nine at the dance, held in our gym, with our brother school Carey. He had braces and we 'pashed' for most of the night while our chaperones looked on. Our one and only date was on a Friday night where we met under the clocks at Flinders Street Station. We didn't *see* much of the movie, due to more 'pashing'. I decided there was no longevity in this relationship because my lips were shredded from his braces.

I was never unhappy in this Enid Blyton world because I was unable to be anything other than happy. I was born sunny side up. But I learned early on that it doesn't pay to be exuberant and diligent and good. Well, it is in the eyes of the teachers but the power of the pack is much more forceful therefore it becomes necessary, for survival, to rein in these qualities for fear of recrimination. It has taken me almost thirty years to regain the things that I tamed in those six years.

Each year, I have returned to Tralfamadore to say hello, stay a while and swim in the river. It continues to hold a spell over me that will never break even if I were never to go back.

The echoes of laughter at the river are faded now and the bush is slowly reclaiming many of the houses. Only a handful of the original 'Tralfamadorians' visit the place. The rest have moved on to other lives and most likely view it as a phase of their life when they lived hippy ideals.

The river house still stands and will give sanctuary for many years to come. The best place to sleep remains in the mezzanine behind the fireplace, up in the trees with the possums. If you lie there with the barn doors open to the sky, you can hear the river talking to the creek and you will learn many, many exceptional secrets. Your ravenous heart will swell and you will sink into sleep with deep exhalations unlike any you have known before.

Acknowledgements

My life is blessed with so many people to enrich it and while my family may have different memories to mine for this period in life, I have come to realise that memory is a trickster and how we each view events can be so different. I don't apologise for mixing things up or playing with time. I'd like to thank Sara, Bill(y) and Jan (Couzie) for sharing the journey on this unconventional childhood.

To Mama, who is anything but conventional, for giving me the gift of story and taking us to Tralfamadore.

To Kev, who has shared a life with me for thirty-two years, and supports all of my hare-brained ideas with love and humour. I love you, Hun. To my sons, Dylan and Jack, I can't imagine life without you – you are my inspiration. You have both grown into the type of men that this world needs: creative, loving and respectful.

And Joe, although these stories come from before we knew you, never think that you aren't part of the fabric of our family.

Carole and Tom for treating me as their own daughter and humouring me in my pursuits. Tom, we miss you every day.

In my writing journey, thank you to the Mud Writing Group – Michele, Lynne, Kim, Mandy and Carol – for workshopping many of these stories and helping me to grow in confidence as a writer for the past ten years. Also, my other writing group: Beau Hillier, Les Zigomanis, Gina Boothroyd, Tess Evans, Deb Bouchier, Angus Watson and Jasmine Powell, for your feedback.

To Inga Simpson for your honest appraisal of an earlier draft of this book, that allowed me to see it in a better light.

And finally to Les Zigomanis: without your love, support, honest feedback, mentorship, and editing there would be no book – thank you.

Author's Note

Kurt Vonnegut created Tralfamadore in his fictional novel, *Slaughterhouse Five*, which was first published in 1969. The Tralfamadore of this memoir was named after the novel as homage to the ideals of the fictional story, the place being a utopian ideal. I would like to thank the estate of Kurt Vonnegut for seeing my story as a homage and fair use of the word. There are many references to literature in these stories because the reading of them shaped my imagination. I thank all these creators for giving me a rich, imaginative childhood.

Printed in Australia
AUHW020830281022
370844AU00005B/15